simply romantic®

DATES on a DIME

FAMILYLIFE®
Help for today. Hope for tomorrow.

Little Rock, Arkansas

DATES ON A DIME
FamilyLife Publishing®
5800 Ranch Drive
Little Rock, Arkansas 72223
1-800-FL-TODAY • FamilyLife.com
FLTI, d/b/a FamilyLife®, is a ministry of Campus Crusade for Christ
International®

ISBN: 978-1-57229-906-1
©2006 FamilyLife

Printed in the United States of America

14 13 12 11 10   4 5 6 7

Contents

Introduction

Try this simple exercise with your spouse tonight: Ask "What is romantic to you?" Listen carefully. Next, share how you describe romance.

We doubt either of you will say "a $500 bottle of perfume," "a new car," or "two-dozen long-stemmed red roses in a crystal vase." Those things are nice, but how many of us can afford them?

The truth is that romance doesn't have to be expensive. It's about thoughtfulness, time together, and the right word at the right time. You simply need forethought and a little creativity.

So if you're short on these, take a look inside. We wrote this book for you. You don't need to try every date, and you may need to adapt them to fit your spouse's idea of romance. Just let these simple suggestions get you started.

Now go ahead, ask the question ...

Fun 'n' Free
Dates

Enjoy a late night swim with your loved one
at a nearby lake or pool.

At your local Humane Society, snuggle and scratch adorable adoptables. Talk about the pets you had as a child. List their names, antics, and habits.

TIP: Commit to waiting 24 hours before deciding to bring a pet home.

On the Fourth of July, grab a blanket and your sweetheart. Find a secluded spot to view the local fireworks display.

Cuddle up in the corner of your library with an
art book or short story that interests both of you.
Choose a color, image, or word and kiss
each time you run across it.

Using your best china, dine by candlelight at home.
Remember to keep it simple:
serve a meal from the grocer's freezer case.

Pack up your laptop and favorite romantic DVD.
Get out to a quiet spot, then cuddle up
and watch the movie.

MONEY $AVING TIP

Join a baby-sitting co-op in your neighborhood or
church. For the hours you sit, you'll earn points to
spend on your nights out for "free" childcare. To
start a co-op, google "baby-sitting co-op" for tips
and suggestions.

At Christmastime, pack your car with a thermos of hot cocoa and two travel mugs. Drive through local neighborhoods, sipping your cocoa and viewing the Christmas light displays. Toast each other when you've found the most outrageous display.

Enjoy complimentary concerts at churches
and schools. Check your local newspaper
for a listing of these and other free events.

APPRECIATION DATE!
Take time to verbalize appreciation for each other.
Note his or her inner qualities and physical beauty.

Visit a home improvement store.
Thumb through the books of house plans
and discuss your dream home.

Most museums offer free admission on certain days. Visit, then bring home a postcard or trinket from the gift shop as a memento.

Picnic at the beach or at a romantic spot nearby.
Burn tea lights at your site, setting them in clear
baby-food jars or other windproof containers.
Don't forget the matches!

Sign up and take a free class at the
local home improvement or garden store.
Then apply your new skills at home.

MONEY $AVING TIP

Search the newspaper, phone book, or websites for
money-saving coupons—especially for restaurants.

Parades are free—and a lot of fun.
At small-town affairs, you'll enjoy spotting friends
and family in the band and on the floats. While you
may not spot friends in the big city, the floats will
be larger than life! Big or little, you can't lose.

simply romantic

Attend a children's sporting event; they're usually free. Watch closely so that by the game's end, you can privately nominate the Most Valuable Player or Most Enthusiastic Soccer Mom.

Stay in and play a creative version
of your favorite card game.

There's no charge on window-shopping!
Visit the mall and model a stunning evening gown
for him or a dashing suit for her. Admire the look,
then kindly place it back on the rack.

Find a private location and sunbathe.
Bring coconut-scented oil and apply
liberally to each other.

simply romantic

21

MONEY $AVING TIP
Empty your pocket change into a jar each night.
Then once a month,
spend your stash on "date night."

SUPER-SIMPLE CAMPFIRE

Bring a bag of ready-to-light charcoal briquettes
and matches to a local campsite or park. Use it to
fuel an evening of snuggling and cozy chatting.

Check your Sunday paper for a listing of
open houses. As you visit each one,
note your favorite features as idea-starters
for future home improvements.

Go parking in a secluded place.
You have a license for this kind of thing—
for driving and marriage and so forth!

Take the rough out of "roughing it."
For just one evening, camp in your backyard.
Skip the tent so you can view the stars.

Volunteer to do an elderly person's yard work.
Sometimes reaching out to others can bring
you together like nothing else can.

Test-drive your fantasy car together.

Take time for a quiet stroll together through
moonlit snow or during a light rain.

BODY ART

Mix 1 egg yolk, 1/2 tsp. water, and a drop
or two of food coloring. Paint each other
and create temporary tattoos.

The best time to star gaze is during the Perseids,
which peak August 12 or 13, and the Geminds,
which peak the nights of December 13 or 14.
For more info see
amsmeteors.org/showers

During the spring or summer, pick wildflowers.
Gather a bouquet for your nightstand and,
if you still remember how,
weave a clover or daisy chain for her.

Use sidewalk chalk to declare your love:
When you stroll through town or down a paved
trail, leave a testament of your love by etching
your initials into a heart with an arrow through it.
As you make your way home on this same path,
stop and kiss at each marker you've created.

Ten-Dollar
Dates

Arm yourselves with one five-dollar bill each.
Then, separately, cruise the aisles of the dollar
store for gifts for each other. Meet up in the car,
where you can exchange gifts and kisses.

Don't miss a trip to the pumpkin patch this fall.
Decorate your front door
or hearth with your fun finds.

Shop the grocery store together for a few favorite dessert toppings. Build and share your own special sundae.

Enjoy community theatre at a fraction
of the price of a Broadway production.

39

The zoo can be a fun and economical
way to spend quality time together.

Pick berries at a u-pick farm.
On the following Saturday morning,
treat yourselves to fresh blueberry pancakes
or strawberry-topped Belgian waffles.

Monday is often a discount day at
the state or county fair. Share some
cotton candy and a funnel cake!

Most communities have a farmer's market
in the summer and fall. Purchase some
fresh veggies while enjoying the outdoors.

43

Play a birthday prank! When a close friend hits
a landmark birthday, sneak out late that night
and mark his land with scads of plastic forks or
pink flamingos. Or, using a glass marker or soap,
post your congratulations on his vehicle windows.

Eat cheap at an all-night diner.

45

Rent a movie, pop some popcorn,
and enjoy the show!

With a cup of coffee in hand, visit the travel
section of a bookstore. Plan your dream vacation.

Digital scavenger hunt—and you're the booty!
As you visit fun places in your town or city,
ask passers-by to snap photos of you and
your honey in these places.

Split an entrée at your favorite local restaurant.

At a local thrift shop and with a budget
of five dollars each, purchase silly souvenirs
commemorating your time together.

Try your hand at pool. With a ten-dollar budget you might be able to afford a snack.

simply romantic

MONEY $AVING TIP
When eating out, order water as
your beverage of choice—it's usually free.

Purchase the fixings for pizza and spend time
in the kitchen making it together.

simply romantic

Using a roll of quarters, create a
vending machine meal for two. Extra points
if you can score all four food groups!

Movie matinees are usually less crowded—
which means you can choose a seat in the
back row and steal a few kisses.

Search out local attractions that you may not
already know about: planetariums, arboretums,
walking trails, etc. Have fun discovering together.

Treat yourselves to an ice cream sundae.
Consider sharing one.

MONEY $AVING TIP

Invest in your marriage by planning a monthly
date night and including the cost in your budget.

Restaurant portions are huge! Skip the entrée
and go for appetizers and drinks.

Spend time together at a coffee house.
You can find lots of coffee-date ideas in
Coffee Dates for Couples.

State and national parks are affordable.
Pack a lunch and enjoy the great outdoors.

61

Most cities and many neighborhoods offer inexpensive and fun festivals. Google "festival" and your city's name for ideas and schedules.

MONEY $AVING TIP

Consider double- or triple-dating where group rates
apply. You can save money and double your fun!

Compete with each other at the driving range
or miniature golf course. Winner buys
the post-game refreshments.

Since you're all dressed up, leave the holiday
party early to share dessert at a swanky
restaurant. Don't forget to tip generously;
your server would have made more money
on a couple eating a full meal.

65

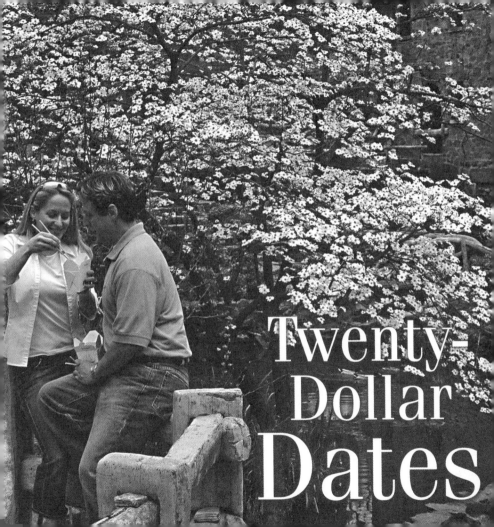

Twenty-Dollar Dates

When the carnival comes to town,
make some memories. Ride the rides, buy some
snacks, and try your hand at the games.

Feel daring? Shop for a new piece of
lingerie together—something you both like.
Ladies, model it that evening.

Consider an easy, lazy, weekend brunch—
lots of food at a reasonable price.

Go go-carting! Last one in the pit gets
the ice cream flavor of choice
at a "pit stop" on the way home.

MONEY $AVING TIP

You'll find that most events are cheaper
in the daytime. Schedule more dates with
your mate when the sun is shining.

Google "drive-in theater." Most states still have a few of these fifties-era fun spots. Box up some snacks and a blanket and head over. It will be worth the drive.

73

Plan a progressive dinner. Share an appetizer
at one eatery, an entrée at another, and finish
by splitting dessert elsewhere.

Check the yellow pages for a
"paint your own pottery" studio. Spend time
creating a memorable piece for your collection.

75

Rent a paddleboat at a nearby lake.
Don't forget to pack a picnic lunch or dinner.

Find a restaurant that serves high tea.
Pretend you are the rulers of your own kingdom.
How would you treat your subjects?

simply romantic

Order Chinese takeout
and dine in a fun and interesting place.
Write your own fortunes for each other.

Use Friday morning's paper to map the local
garage sales. Then on Saturday morning,
shop with a budget of twenty dollars.
Purchase something special for your home.

Purchase two tickets to a minor league baseball
or arena football game. Take your own peanuts.

Rent a convertible for the day and take
a long, leisurely, scenic drive.

Scout out a walking tour in or near your city.
Learn something new together.

Enjoy drama or sporting events
on a local college campus.

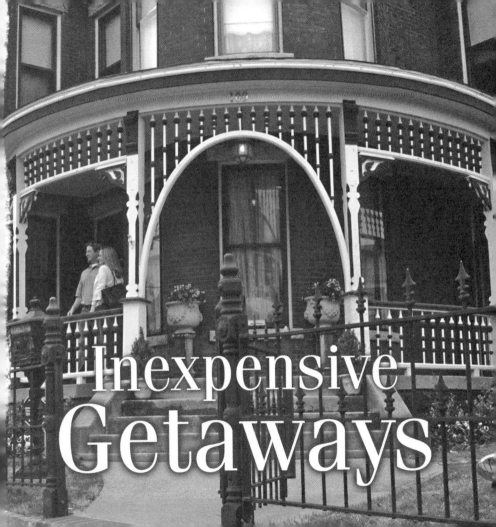

Inexpensive Getaways

Grab or borrow camping gear and head for the hills. Spend the weekend enjoying the outdoors and each other.

86

Take advantage of the weekend specials that most hotels offer. Get a room with a hot tub and BYOBB (bring your own bubble bath).

MONEY $AVING TIP

Find ways to collect points that can be redeemed
for free flights and hotel rooms. Then cash them
in on a trip for the two of you—alone.

House-sit for friends or family
while they are out of town. Make it a
special "getaway" without leaving town.

If you or your spouse travel for business, take the trip together. You'll save on lodging expenses— and transportation if you drive instead of fly.

Rent a cabin in the off-season. Take along groceries to save on the cost of eating out.

Send the kids to Grandma's house for the weekend.
Turn your home into "Fantasy Island."

MONEY $AVING TIP
Check out your employee benefits packages.
They might include special rates
on theme parks, hotels, etc.

The Hospitality Club will help you find people who will host you in their homes. Membership is usually free. See hospitalityclub.org for more information.

Ask friends and church members if any own
a vacation or weekend home. Arrange to rent
or borrow it for the weekend.

95

Take a trip down memory lane. Arrange to spend a few days at your childhood home.

Plan a mini-vacation with another couple—
sharing the expense of lodging and the
work of cooking and cleaning up.

Steal away to a bed and breakfast during the week.
The rates are lower than those on weekends.

Some monasteries and convents open their
doors to guests for little or no charge.
Spend time praying for your marriage.

My Cheap Date Ideas

My Cheap Date Ideas

Love like you mean it. At FamilyLife's Weekend to Remember marriage getaway, you can put aside life's daily distractions and focus on each other again. For over thirty years, we've helped over a million couples make their marriages stronger and healthier.

FAMILYLIFE presents
weekend to
remember

FamilyLife.com/Weekend • 1-800-FL-TODAY

Fan the flames of romance!

Tips to Romance Your Husband and *Tips to Romance Your Wife* bring spark and sizzle to your marriage. Learn to communicate heart-to-heart, express love through food and fun, give gifts that say I love you, and romance your love on birthdays and holidays. Heat up your marriage with these creative ideas and become *Simply Romantic!*

Warm up your love life with satisfying and memorable coffeehouse moments.

Join your spouse in smooth, full-bodied conversations that blend stimulating depth and a soulful connection.

Coffee Dates for Couples provides refreshing conversation starters and flavorful date ideas. Your coffee experience will be renewed and recharged, as you enjoy the rich aroma of a robust, spicy conversation with your spouse in the haven of java!

Order today at 1-800-FL-TODAY (358-6329), 24 hours a day, or visit FamilyLife.com

Looking for a little sizzle?

Simply Romantic Nights® collections are designed to put the wow! back into marriage. These romance resources are filled with innovative ideas to kindle sensational encounters and encourage intimacy. Both sets include 24 unique romantic-adventure cards (12 cards for him, 12 for her) with complete plans for creative dates, plus a companion book and more.

Simply add your personal touch, build anticipation…and let the sparks fly!

Order yours today at 1-800-FL-TODAY or FamilyLife.com/SimplyRomantic